QUANTUM MECHANICS!

THE HOW'S AND WHY'S OF ATOMS AND MOLECULES

CHEMISTRY FOR KIDS

CHILDREN'S CHEMISTRY BOOKS

pfiffikus

EDUCATIONAL BOOKS FOR CHILDREN K-12

Do atoms and molecules mean the same thing? Are atoms made of molecules? Which is which?

The fact is that molecules are made of atoms. When two atoms join together, they form a molecule. The fact is that molecules are made of atoms. When two atoms join together, they form a molecule.

Do you know that everything is made up of atoms? A pen, the TV you watch, the video game you play are formed by atoms. You, too, are formed by atoms. Trillions of different types of molecules are in us. Atoms come in over 100 different kinds.

The word atom means "uncuttable" in Greek. It just means that atoms are impossible to divide into smaller units. It was believed that they are the smallest unit or the basic unit of matter, although now we know there are sub-atomic particles.

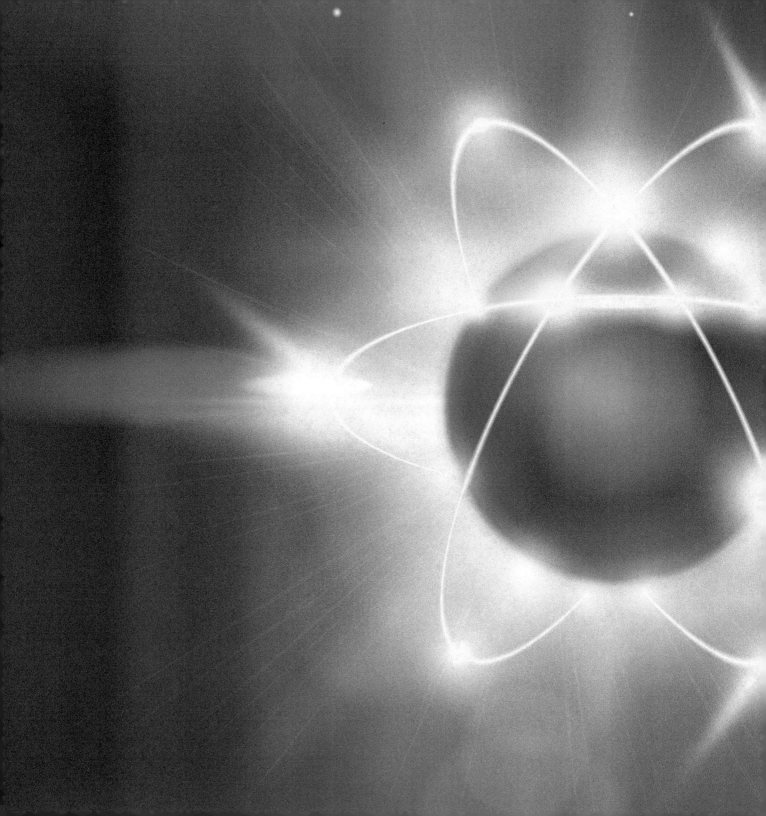

An atom has at its core the nucleus. It is made up of subatomic particles known as neutrons and protons. Electrons are the tiny particles that move around the nucleus at amazing speeds.

Atoms are the smallest unit of an element. Yet, they contain tinier particles. These are called quarks and leptons. Electrons are leptons.

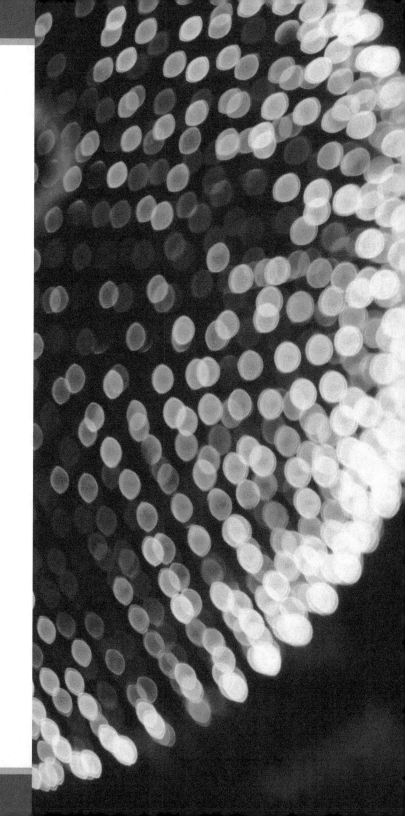

Atoms bond together and molecules are formed. Everything around us is composed of molecules.

An atom's individual structure will determine how many other atoms it can bond to.

Atoms build molecules or form materials. Larger particles form when atoms connect together through chemical bonds. To form these bonds, atoms share and exchange electrons.

The three types of bonds are covalent, metallic and ionic bonds. Electrons are used by atoms to form any of these bonds.

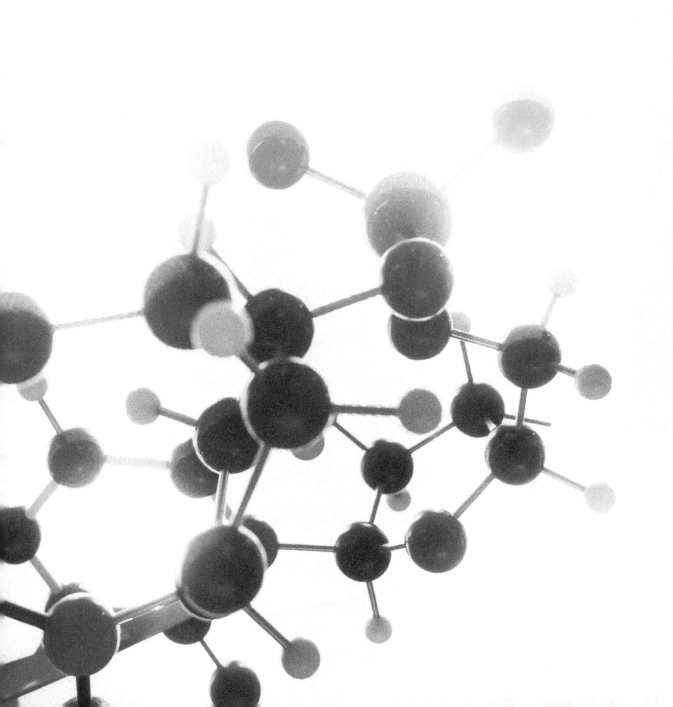

Molecules can hold their atoms together. Covalent bonding is a strong connection between atoms like in carbon dioxide and water; while an ionic bond provides weaker connection of atoms, like in rocks.

The arrangement of bonds that hold the atoms will give the molecule its shape. A carbon dioxide molecule has the chemical formula CO2. This means that it is composed of one carbon atom and two oxygen atoms.

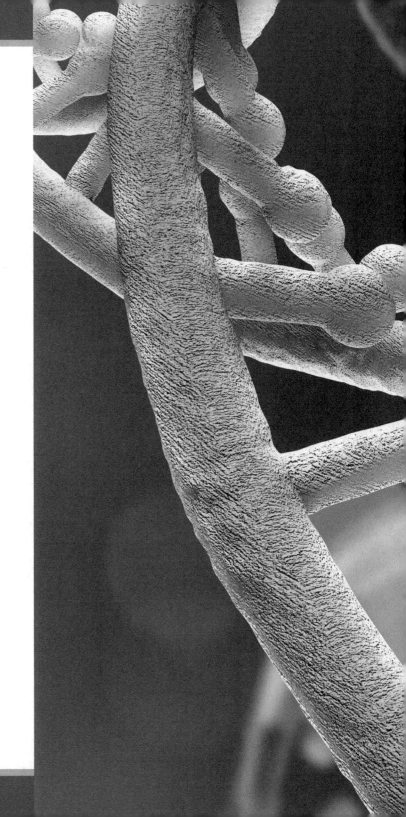

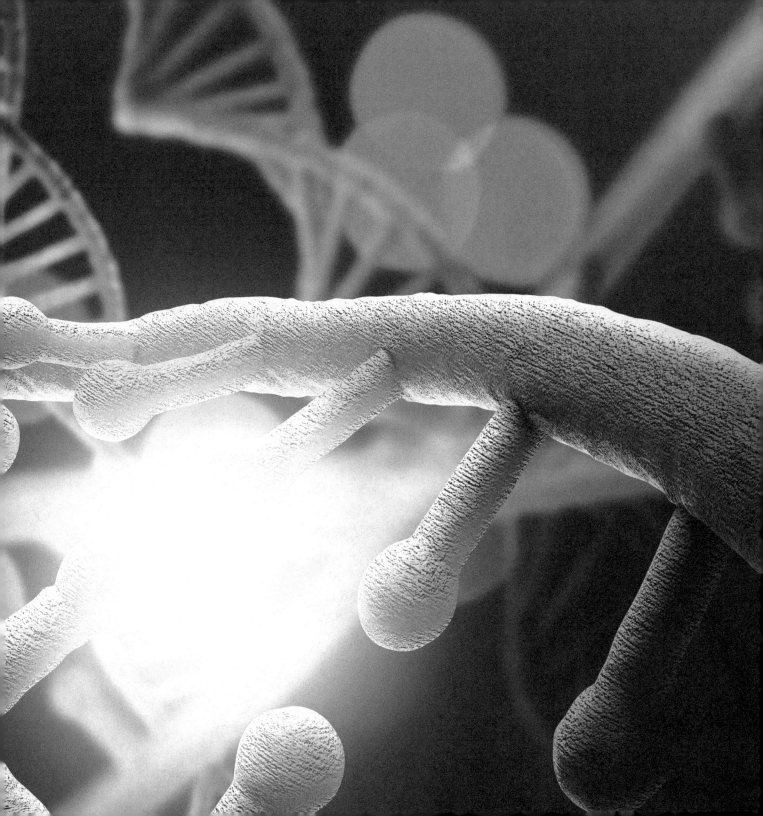

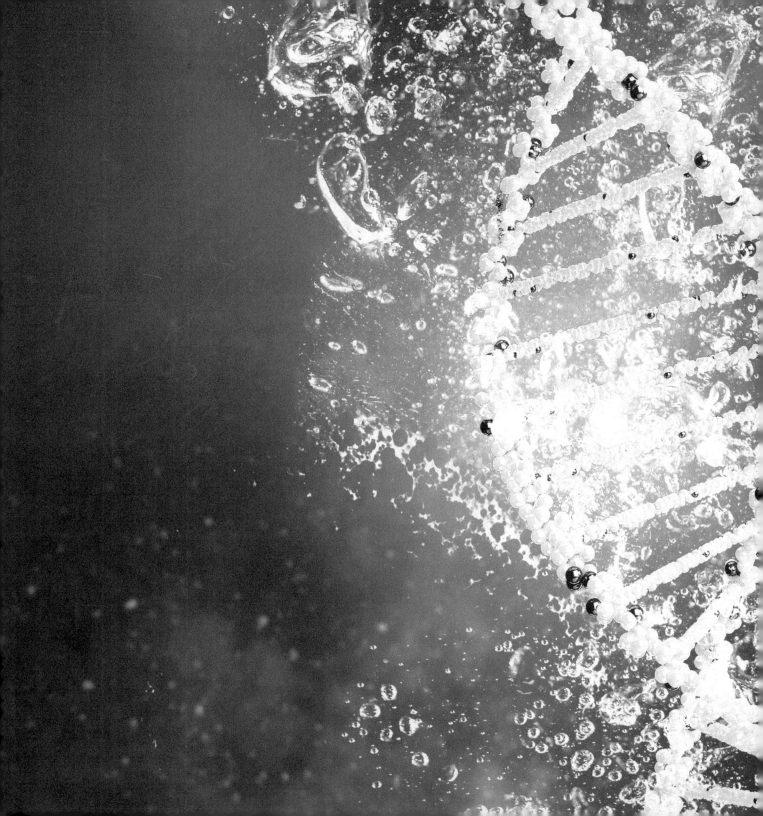

The molecules of compounds contain different types of atoms. Through chemical reactions, molecules are changed. When a molecule joins with other molecules, new compounds can be formed.

Molecules come in simple and complex forms. Some molecules are made of just one atom, like the element argon. Through chemical reactions, new molecules and new compounds are formed as the molecules change and rearrange their atoms.

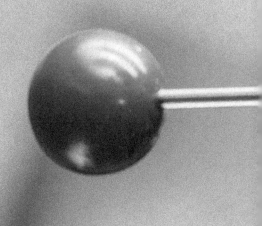

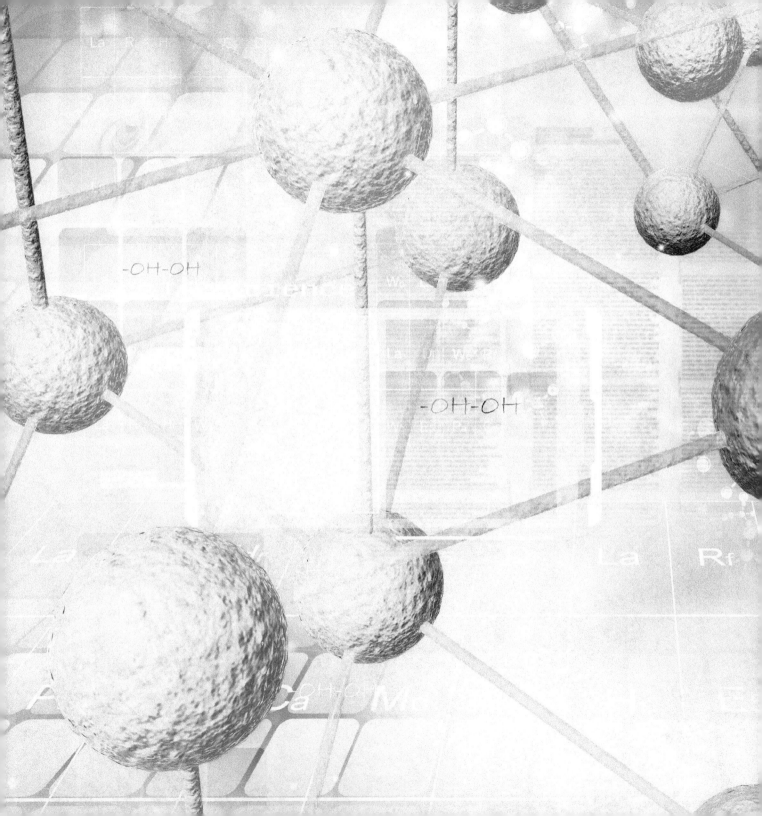

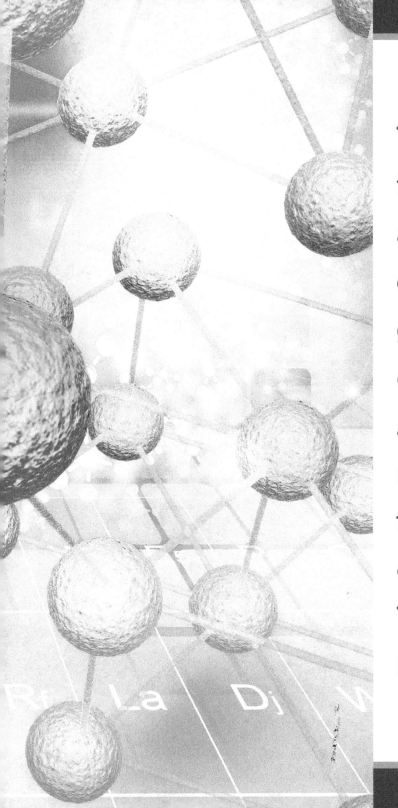

Take the oxygen that we breathe as an example. The oxygen in our body goes through a chemical change. As this happens, a new compound is formed in the form of carbon dioxide. This is what we breathe out.

The manipulation of atoms and molecules in order to produce materials is called nanotechnology. This includes the making of devices and machines. This process starts from small things and moves to big things.

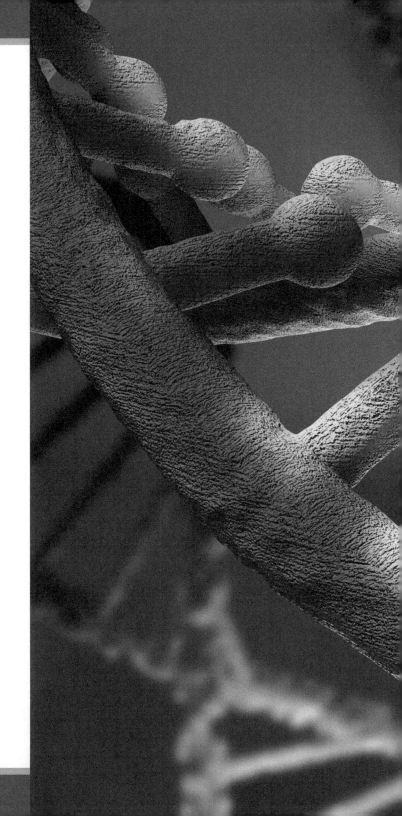

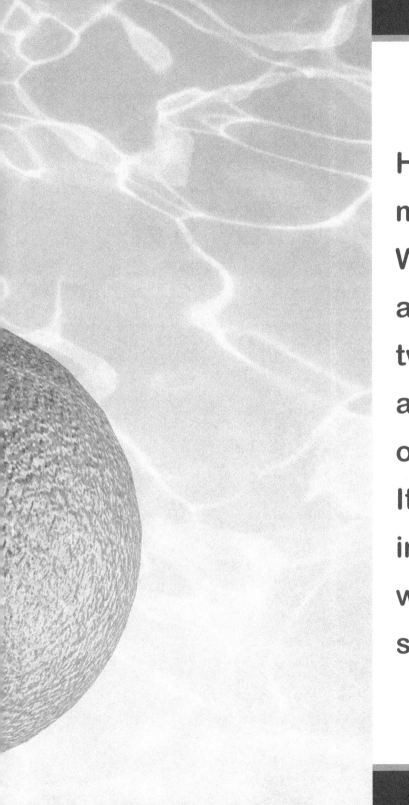

How are water molecules formed? Water molecules are made up of two hydrogen atoms and one oxygen atom: H_2O. It is estimated that in just a drop of water, there are 2 sextillion atoms.

Chemical formulae are the symbols used by scientists to represent molecules.

Atoms of different elements bonded together form compounds. Water is composed of compound molecules. These are 2 hydrogen atoms and 1 oxygen atom. That is why it is labeled as H2O.

CPSIA information can be obtained
at www.ICGtesting.com
Printed in the USA
BVHW010206080620
581073BV00016B/777